CommonMark Ready Reference

For the new MarkDown standard

V. Subhash

CommonMark Ready Reference

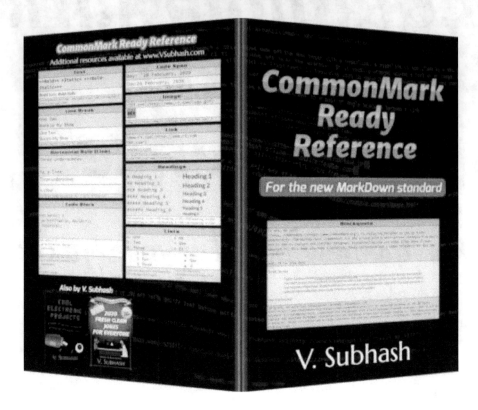

Written and designed by

V. Subhash
(www.VSubhash.in)

Copyright

Preface

Here are a few things you need to know before reading further.

Naming convention

I use the word 'markdown' (in lower case) to refer to any MarkDown implementation, dialect or superset including CommonMark. Specifically, MarkDown means the original MarkDown.

Examples convention

The CommonMark examples are displayed in a `<pre><code>...</code></pre>` block. It has a thick left border. The HTML output of the examples will be in `<blockquote>...</blockquote>` blocks. They will be dashed edges.

Version and dialect

This book is based on Version 0.30 of CommonMark. It may be superseded by newer versions. Whatever the case, the official documentation that came with the version of CommonMark/Markdown that you use in production will always have more relevance.

Although the CommonMark information in this book may apply to MarkDown as well, there are subtle differences between the two. The following text to create a heading passes for MarkDown but not for CommonMark.

```
#FFMPEG Quick Hacks
```

You may be expecting this:

```
FFMPEG Quick Hacks
```

But, it will not be processed by CommonMark and be output as:

```
#FFMPEG Quick Hacks
```

What went wrong? Answer: There has to be a space between the hash and the text. The following is valid CommonMark.

```
# FFMPEG Quick Hacks
```

If something from this book does not work with a markdown processor, you need to refer to its documentation.

Then, there are features not supported by both MarkDown and CommonMark, such as strikethroughs and tables. This book sticks to the reference implementation and will not bother with extended syntax supported by markdown extensions. However, this book will suggest workarounds for the same kind of output without using such extensions.

Purpose

The paperback version of this book is for those who need a desk-side reference and for

 codinghorror ANN: My CommonMark book, some queries, and a wishlist

those who would like to learn CommonMark (or MarkDown) at leisure. The paperback is black-n-white or grayscale. Only the cover is in colour. Hence, both covers have been designed as quick reference cards for MarkDown/CommonMark. In the annexures, a grayscale version of the quick reference card is available. You can remove the page and make as many photocopies as you want. (Cut the page with a blade or a pair of scissors. Do not tug at it and ruin the binding.)

If you are on a computer with an Internet connection, there will be plenty of other free alternatives including the official documentation. The ebook version of this book is for people to decide whether it is worth having the paperback on their desk. (The ebook does not include the quick reference card.) The full-colour covers of the paperback is available as a CommonMark/MarkDown cheat sheet or quick reference card on my website. You can print it on a colour printer. Download it for free from:

http://www.vsubhash.in/commonmark.html

Chapters

MarkDown & CommonMark

In the beginning, there was text. Then, came markup *a la* HTML. After that, came MarkDown.

Before the invention of the WorldWideWeb (WWW), there was Internet. Communication on this pre-WWW Internet was through email, Usenet, and other text-based protocols. To add context to this text messages, some primitive formatting such as bold, italic and underline styles were applied to the text. (In those days, even the computer displays could not display richly formatted text.) This formatting style found new avenues in the era of the WWW. HTML was a **markUP** language. For ease-of-use, security and other reasons, not everyone wanted to deal with markup. This set the stage for the invention of a **markDOWN** language called MarkDown.

> **https://daringfireball.net/projects/markdown/**

MarkDown is a phenomenal success and has been adopted all over the WWW and beyond. (My books are all written in MarkDown, not exported from MS Word. This book is written in CommonMark.) However, MarkDown has begun to show its age. It does not have a well-defined spec. There were several interpretations based on the perl program created for the original MarkDown implementation. MarkDown also gave rise to newer dialects and supersets that added more features. A more codified MarkDown was needed. This is where CommonMark comes from. It hit the road with a well-defined spec. It supports MarkDown but clarifies many of its rules for implementers in unambiguous terms. Many websites including StackOverFlow.com have adopted CommonMark. CommonMark is all set to replace and surpass MarkDown as the *de facto* standard for low-markup text.

> **https://commonmark.org/**

The reference implementation of CommonMark is written in C and is incredibly fast. This is the main reason I like it very much. The older MarkDown used the perl interpreter. While it is good, it is nowhere near as fast.

After the release of version 0.30, the CommonMark specification is considered stable and requiring no further development. If you need CommonMark to support document elements that are not supported by it (such as tables), you can use CommonMark dialects that have extended its syntax. This book sticks to the canonical implementation and suggests raw HTML workarounds for features not supported by it.

Starting with CommonMark

Anyone can build CommonMark from its source code available at
https://github.com/commonmark/cmark. I built my CommonMark executables
(for Linux and Windows) using version 0.30 of the source code.

Build

The following commands download, build and install Linux and Windows variants
of the CommonMark executable. You probably want to create a link to the
`/home/$USERNAME/Builds/CommonMark/linux-bin/bin/cmark` executable file in
your `~/bin` directory so that you can use it in your commands and shell scripts
without typing its full path. The Windows executable `cmark.exe` will be found in
the `/home/$USERNAME/Builds/CommonMark/windows-bin/bin` directory. You can
copy it to a suitable location on your Windows file system in case you would like
to use it in that OS.

```
sudo apt-get install build-essential mingw-w64 unzip curl

mkdir -p ~/Builds/CommonMark/cmark-bin-linux
mkdir -p ~/Builds/CommonMark/cmark-bin-windows
cd ~/Builds/CommonMark

curl --output cmark-src.zip \
  --location \
  https://github.com/commonmark/cmark/archive/refs/heads/master.zip

unzip cmark-src.zip
mv cmark-master cmark-src

cd cmark-src
make INSTALL_PREFIX="$HOME/Builds/CommonMark/cmark-bin-linux"
make test

make install

make clean
make mingw \
    MINGW_INSTALLDIR="$HOME/Builds/CommonMark/cmark-bin-windows"
```

Windows developers can build the executable following the instructions at the
source code site. The Linux and Windows executables that I had built are available
on my website. You can use them at your own risk.

> http://www.vsubhash.in/commonmark.html

Usage

In the past, I used the MarkDown perl script from daringfireball.net for building
my books. The command that I used was:

```
perl Markdown.pl book.md > book.html
```

For CommonMark Linux executable, I use:

```
cmark --unsafe --validate-utf8 book.md > book.html
```

The `--unsafe` option is necessary for me because I use a few HTML blocks in my MarkDown/CommonMark documents. Because I wrote the HTML, I trust it. If you are using CommonMark on a production system, you are expected to disinfect the HTML code to prevent XSS attacks.

If I were a MS Windows user, I would have tried:

```
cmark.exe --unsafe --validate-utf8 book.md > book.html
```

Installation and use in Apache/PHP

```
sudo apt install php-pear php7.4-dev libcmark-dev

# Point pear to your PHP initialization file
pear config-set php_ini /etc/php/7.4/apache2/php.ini

sudo pear install cmark-1.2.0.tgz
# After downloading from
# https://pecl.php.net/package/cmark

sudo service apache2 restart
```

Check you code with:

```
<?php

$sMarkDown="**Hello, World!**";
$oNode = CommonMark\Parse($sMarkDown);
echo CommonMark\Render\HTML($oNode);

?>
```

If you are using the methods in your own namespaces or class, do remember to rewrite the code as:

```
$sMarkDown="**Hello, World!**";
$oNode = \CommonMark\Parse($sMarkDown);
echo \CommonMark\Render\HTML($oNode);
```

By default, the extension omits any raw HTML found in the markdown. To get around it, use a different overload of the HTML-rendering method.

```
define("CMARK_OPT_UNSAFE", (1 << 17));

...

$oCmDoc = \CommonMark\Parse($asMarkdown);
$sHtml = \CommonMark\Render\HTML($oCmDoc, CMARK_OPT_UNSAFE);
```

Text

There are people who prefer to read email only in plain text. They set their email clients to convert HTML email to plain text. What do you think is displayed when this conversion is done? Some sort of markdown! Essentially, email clients do the the reverse of MarkDown.

Bold

```
**FFMPEG Quick Hacks** by V. Subhash
__FFMPEG Quick Hacks__ by V. Subhash
```

FFMPEG Quick Hacks by V. Subhash

Italic

```
*FFMPEG Quick Hacks* by V. Subhash
_FFMPEG Quick Hacks_ by V. Subhash
```

FFMPEG Quick Hacks by V. Subhash

Bold-italic

```
What did the regular font say to the bold type? "You are
***grotesque***!"
What did the regular font say to the bold type? "You are
___grotesque___!"
```

What did the regular font say to the bold type? "You are ***grotesque***!"

Strikethrough

There is no support for strikethrough. (Some markdown processors support text wrapped in double tildes (~~) for strikethrough.) You will have to use the HTML tag `<s>` or `<del>`. The text wrapped in an HTML tag will not be processed by markdown. If the output is HTML, this is fine. It may not be so with other output formats. If you are using the HTML for further processing, say for EPUB ebook generation (which requires strict XHTML), then `<s>` cannot be used.

```
I <s>studied hardly</s> for the exam.
I <del>studied hardly</del> for the exam.
```

I ~~studied hardly~~ for the exam.

Paragraphs

All adjacent lines containing plain text will be converted to a paragraph or `<p>` tag in the HTML output.

```
The mistake was in not forbidding the serpent; then he would
have eaten the serpent.
```

> The mistake was in not forbidding the serpent; then he would have eaten the serpent.

Text can be separated by an empty line. It will create a new paragraph.

```
He did not want the apple for the apple's sake.

He wanted it only because it was forbidden.
```

> He did not want the apple for the apple's sake.
>
> He wanted it only because it was forbidden.

If there is no double space or backslash [\ ] at the end of a line and the next line is not empty, the text continues as one paragraph.

```
Adam was but human.
This explains it all.
```

> Adam was but human. This explains it all.

I had the Mark Twain lines butchered in reverse.

Line breaks

A backslash [\ ] at the end of the line will insert a line break. In the HTML output, it will continue to be part of the same `<p>` tag. A `<br />` tag will be added to create the break.

```
One two\
Buckle my show
```

> One two\
> Buckle my show

Two space characters can also be use in place of the backslash but as you cannot see them at the end of the line, I recommend that you do not use them.

Inline code

Inline code is usually rendered using even-width font. (The text gets wrapped in a `<code>` span). To output inline code, you need to place the text between a pair of backquotes or backticks [`].

```
The keyword `register` is not used anymore.
```

> The keyword `register` is not used anymore.

Sometimes, at the end of a line, your delicately carved dollop of code goodness will break. There is a HTML work around for it. Wrap it up like this: `<code style="white-space: nowrap; ">Unbreakable Code</code>`. Better create a CSS class with it.

As opposed to inline code span, a code block (described in a **separate chapter** begins with three backticks. Here is a challenge: How can you output three backticks in a code span if you wanted to demonstrate it to someone? Should you use five consecutive backticks (`````)? No, wrap them with two backticks and a space on either side.

```
A code block begins with three backticks (`` ``` ``).
```

> A code block begins with three backticks (```).

One leading and trailing space will be removed.

Escaping

A backslash before any ASCI punctuation character will disable the usual Markdown/CommonMark treatment.

```
*Italic*
**Bold**
\*Not Italic\*
\*\*Not bold\*\*
Backslash (\\)
What Backslash (\)
\* Options marked with an asterisk are not optional.
* Options marked with what are not optional.
```

> *Italic*
> **Bold**
> *Not Italic*
> **Not bold**
> Backslash (\)
> What Backslash ()
> * Options marked with an asterisk are not optional.
> - Options marked with what are not optional.

The backslash can also be escaped with a backslash. This sort of escaping does not apply to code or HTML blocks.

```
I cannot remember the difference. Backlash (\\) seems to be
laidback. Forward slash (/) looks like it is about to fall
forward. Just like *fall forward* and *spring back*. Confusing
when you can also *spring forward* and *fall back*.
```

I cannot remember the difference. Backlash (\\) seems to be laidback. Forward slash (/) looks like it is about to fall forward. Just like *fall forward* and *spring back*. Confusing when you can also *spring forward* and *fall back*.

Images

You specify an image by its location. An alternate description is recommended to support accessibility applications, which will use the text to describe the image to people with disabilities. When the image is loading or fails to load, this description text will also provide a clue about its purpose in the image placeholder box. The title attribute (hover text) is displayed by web browsers when the mouse hovers over the image.

Inline images

The markdown for an image begins with an exclamation mark. Then, in a pair of square brackets following it, you specify the alternate description for the image. Then, in a pair of curved brackets, you specify the absolute or relative location of the image. You can also specify a quoted title attribute (hover text) in the curved brackets after the image location.

```
![Loading](./images/ani-ajax-wait.gif "Please wait..")
```

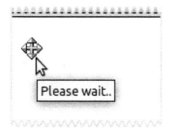

Referenced images

The images can also be specified by reference. The reference is defined just once in the document with the URL of the image. Any number of instances of that image can be created using that reference. After the image instances are created, markdown will discard the reference. There will be no trace of it in the output.

```
![Loading][arrow_animation]

...

![Searching][arrow_animation]

...

[arrow_animation]: ./images/ani-ajax-wait.gif "Please wait"
```

This markdown creates two image instances using the reference `[arrow_animation]`. At the end of the document, the reference is defined with a colon, a space, the URL and the optional title text.

Captioned images

In HTML, there is a new *FIGURE* tag with an encapsulated *FIGURECAPTION* tag. The *IMG* tag is placed inside it.

```
<figure>
  <img src="./photo-zbigniew-brzezinski.jpg" alt="Photo of
Zbigniew Brzezinski" />
  <figcaption>Confessed to provoking an invasion</figcaption>
</fiture>
```

Using CSS, the tag can be styled like a box. The image description below the image can be styled like a paragraph bounded by the box. Unfortunately CommonMark does not generate *FIGURE* tags. It continues to wrap *IMG* tags inside a *P* tag. However, if you can use Javascript, there is an easy workaround. You can find the code on my blog:

http://www.vsubhash.in/blogs/blog/2022-12-02-a-commonmark-
markdown-workaround-for-creating-figure-and-figcaption-tags.html

What it requires is adding a quoted title attribute after the image URL. This will serve as the caption. The Javascript will then insert a *FIGURE* tag version of the image and delete the original image tag and its wrapping paragraph tag. The title attribute will be used as the text content for the *FIGURECAPTION* tag. If the image was part a link (as explained in the next chapter), then the figure caption will be automatically hyperlinked. This workaround neatly avoids using any hacks in the markdown.

```
[![Photo of Zbigniew Brzezinski](./photo-zbigniew-
brzezinski.jpg "Confessed to provoking an invasion")]
(https://williamblum.org/essays/read/how-the-us-provoked-the-
soviet-union-into-invading-afghanistan-and-starting "William
Blum: How the US provoked the Soviet Union into invading
Afghanistan and starting the whole mess")
```

The first screenshot below shows how the above markdown will be displayed as HTML. The image tag is wrapped inside a paragraph tag as always. The second and third screenshot how the paragraph tag has been eliminated by a figure–and–figcation tag combination. The last screenshot shows how the caption has been hyperlinked. Both the image and hyperlink have repurposed title attributes.

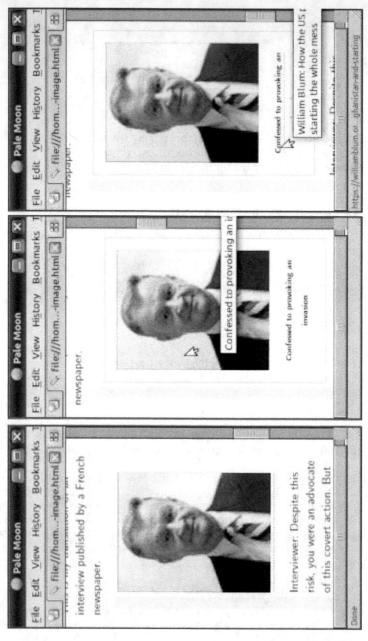

Links

The WWW began with a hyperlink. A hyperlink is specified by a URL (Uniform Resource Locator or the address). It is usually wrapped around a text or an image. A title attribute (hover text) is typically used to describe what happens when the end-user clicks the link.

Just the URL

A URL in a pair of angle brackets becomes a link.

```
<http://www.vsubhash.in>
<mailto:foo@bar.com>
<irc://irc.freenode.net/ffmpeg>
```

> **http://www.vsubhash.in**
> **mailto:foo@bar.com**
> **irc://irc.freenode.net/ffmpeg**

If the link has a space, replace it with %20. For example, write <http://example.com/my page.html> as **http://example.com/my%20page.html**.

Text link

Place the link text between square brackets and the URL between curved brackets.

```
[www.VSubhash.in](http://www.vsubhash.in/)
```

> **www.VSubhash.in**

Text link with title attribute

The quoted text string after the URL is the title attribute (hover text).

```
[www.VSubhash.in](http://www.vsubhash.in/ "Visit my site")
```

> **www.VSubhash.in**

Image link

Write the markdown for an image in the square brackets of a link where you would normally specify the link text.

Do not specify the title attribute (hover text) for the image because you need to specify one for the link. This is for the sake of prudence, not that CommonMark or MarkDown will object.

```
[![www.vsubhash.com](http://www.vsubhash.in/sss-img/banner-
vsubhash-dotcom220.png)](http://www.vsubhash.com/ "Visit my
site")
```

Reference links

Like image references, multiple hyperlink instances can be created using one link
reference, specified in a second set of square brackets.

```
My website is at [www.VSubhash.in][1]. It has lots of articles…

…

To visit the site, click [here][1].

…

[1]: http://www.vsubhash.in/
```

My website is at **www.VSubhash.in**. It has lots of articles…

…

To visit the site, click **here**.

…

The [1] reference can be any arbitrary text. I have used [1] to make it look like it
is part of a list of citations.

Thus, a link reference should be defined once and only once in the markdown and
set to a URL (address).

After the link instances are created, markdown extinguishes the reference. In
other words, the reference does not appear anywhere in the output document.

Reference links for citations

When you write citations, you would want the references to be retained in the
document. But, MarkDown/CommonMark will remove them after the links are
created. When I wrote my article on vintage radio, I was faced with this problem
and I devised this HTML workaround.

```
By the [1920s][nbc], commercial radio networks run by the
National Broadcasting Corporation (NBC) had become popular.
Although the television was invented in the 1930s, it did not
take off as factories and materials were diverted for war
production. Thus, radio enjoyed two decades as the most popular
```

```
medium for news and entertainment. These decades are known as
the *[golden age of radio][golden_age]*. After World War II, TV
displaced radio in popularity. Radio then served a niche -
people on their commute. In the age of the Internet...

...

[nbc]: #nbc
[golden_age]: #golden_age

---

###### References

   * <span id="nbc"></span>
     National Broadcasting Company history files -
<https://lccn.loc.gov/2002660093>
   * <span id="golden_age"></span>
     Golden Age of American radio -
<http://www.britannica.com/topic/Golden-Age-of-American-radio>
```

By the **1920s**, commercial radio networks run by the National Broadcasting
Corporation (NBC) had become popular. Although the television was invented
in the 1930s, it did not take off as factories and materials were diverted for
war production. Thus, radio enjoyed two decades as the most popular medium
for news and entertainment. These decades are known as the *golden age of
radio*. After World War II, TV displaced radio in popularity. Radio then served
a niche - people on their commute. In the age of the Internet...

...

References

- National Broadcasting Company history files -
  https://lccn.loc.gov/2002660093
- Golden Age of American radio -
  http://www.britannica.com/topic/Golden-Age-of-American-radio

When you create the markdown references, do not use the actual links. Instead,
use relative links to anchors defined in a quite visible citations or references
section.

I have used empty <span> tags with ID attributes serving as anchors. Old-style
<a name="anchor"></a> tags can also be used, except when strict XHTML is
required in downstream processing such as ebook generation.

I have named the anchors with the same name as the references. This is for my
understanding and convenience. It is not a markdown requirement.

You can see this workaround in action on my website at:

http://www.vsubhash.in/vintage-radio-shows.html

Horizontal Rule

A fancy name for a line

Three or more asterisks, hyphens or underscores will create a line.

```
Stay Behind This Line
***
Trespassers will be shot.
```

Stay Behind This Line

Trespassers will be shot.

With a string of hyphens, the preceding line should be empty.

```
Stay Behind This Line

---
Trespassers will be shot.
```

Otherwise, a h2 tag/heading will be created.

Stay Behind This Line
Trespassers will be shot.

For the sake of clarity, I would use an empty line before and after the string of line characters.

```
Stay Behind This Line

___

Trespassers will be shot.
```

How do you get a 1-pixel line like this?

1-pixel

---

line

The default style for a line in many browsers is a fuzzy blurry line. Change it using CSS.

```
hr { height: 0!important; border-style: none!important; border-bottom: 1px solid black!important; }
```

Code blocks

Pre-formatted code block

Three or more backticks (``` ``` ```) or tildes (`~~~`) can be used to start a pre-formatted code block (`<pre><code>...</code></pre>`). Any line starting with four spaces will also be considered as a code block.

```
```
int main() {
  print("Hello, World!");
  return(0);
}
```
```

```
~~~
int main() {
  print("Hello, World!");
  return(0);
}
~~~
```

```
int main() {
  print("Hello, World!");
  return(0);
}
```

```
    int main() {
      print("Hello, World!");
      return(0);
    }
```

Escape three backquotes or tildes

How would you display three backquotes in a markdown document without losing the formatting? Wrap them in a greater number of backquotes or tildes.

```
`````
```
FORMAT A: /Q
```
`````
```

```
    ```
    FORMAT A: /Q
    ```
```

A riskier alternative is to use backquotes and tildes alternatively.

```
```
~~~
FORMAT A: /Q
~~~
```
```

```
    ~~~
    FORMAT A: /Q
    ~~~
```

# Code blocks with language hints

You can specify the language name after the opening string of backquotes.

```
```javascript
window.alert("Hello, World!");
```
```

```
    window.alert("Hello, World!");
```

When output to HTML, the following code block will have a
`class="language-javascript"` attribute added to it.

```
<pre><code class="language-javascript">window.alert("Hello,
World!");
</code></pre>
```

Many syntax-highlighting JavaScript scripts recognize these attributes and style
them accordingly. If not, then you may want to add a
`pre.language-javascript { ... }` style in your CSS.

# Plain pre-formatted text blocks

If you want to write pre-formatted text without a code block, just use `<pre>...`
`</pre>` tags. They will not be processed by markdown.

```
<pre>
                /‾‾‾\
              -------
              |o|o|
              ^^^^^^^
               \ ~ /
               | |
------o00o----------------------------
|              The End              |
```

```
         |                                    |
         ---------------------------o00o------
            | |   | |
            ---   ---
            (_)   (_)
</pre>
```

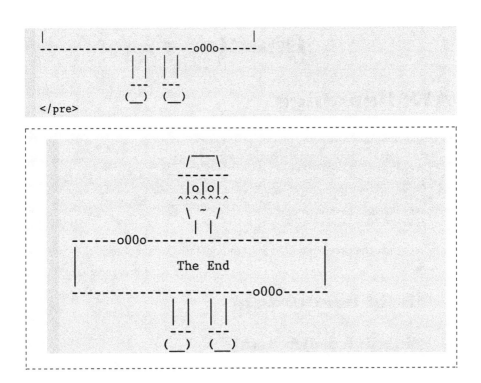

# Headings

## ATX headings

HTML supports headings from size 1 to 6. You can use an equal number of pound or hash symbols before some text to create a heading.

```
# H1 (h1 header tag)
## H2 (h2 header tag)
### H3 (h3 header tag)
#### H4 (h4 header tag)
##### H5 (h5 header tag)
##### H6 (h6 header tag)
```

A space before the text is required in CommonMark but not needed in MarkDown.

# H1 (h1 header tag)

## H2 (h2 header tag)

### H3 (h3 header tag)

#### H4 (h4 header tag)

##### H5 (h5 header tag)

###### H6 (h6 header tag)

## Settext headings

This markdown style is available for the first two heading sizes – H1 and H2.

```
H1 (h1 header tag)
==================

H2 (h2 header tag)
------------------
```

---

# H1 (h1 header tag)

# H2 (h2 header tag)

---

# Adding heading IDs

There is no support for IDs for any tags. (An HTML ID for a heading tag is useful when you want to link to the heading from another location, say, from the Table of Contents.) As always, there is a workaround. Place the HTML anchors inside the header tags.

```
### Inline<a name="images_inline"></a>

### Inline<a id="images_inline"></a>

### Inline<span id="images_inline"></span>
```

Any hyperlink to `#images_inline` will now link to this heading.

```
<h3>Inline<a name="images_inline"></a></h3>

<h3>Inline<a id="images_inline"></a></h3>

<h3>Inline<span id="images_inline"></span></h3>
```

Yes, the headings are quite an eyesore. However, it is effective. If the end-user is only going to see the HTML output, then the looks of the markdown source are not relevant. What they do not know will not hurt them.

If the presence of an anchor inside the heading causes some processing problems, a less elegant solution is to place the anchor right after the heading.

```
### Inline

<a name="images_inline"></a>In the square brackets, you...
```

This results in:

```
<h2>Images</h2>

<p><a name="images_inline"></a>In the square brackets, you...
```

Any hyperlink to `#images_inline` will now link to the content after the heading but not exactly to the heading. Use it only if everything else fails.

# Blockquotes

Blockquote are usually indented and formatted a little differently from the enveloping text. This creates contextual awareness in the reader that this passage might be from another source.

```
In his book *Eve's Diary*, Mark Twain puts a spin on the Eve
and the snake story:

>Adam was but human—this explains it all. He did not want the
apple for the apple's sake, he wanted it only because it was
forbidden. The mistake was in not forbidding the serpent; then
he would have eaten the serpent.

There, it was God's fault!
```

In his book *Eve's Diary*, Mark Twain puts a spin on the Eve and the snake story:

> Adam was but human—this explains it all. He did not want the apple for the apple's sake, he wanted it only because it was forbidden. The mistake was in not forbidding the serpent; then he would have eaten the serpent.

There, it was God's fault!

# One quoted line - one paragraph

A blockquote begins with an angle bracket.

```
Here is an extract from my vintage radio article.
>Mel Blanc was the voice behind popular cartoon characters such
as Daffy Duck, Bugs Bunny, Porky Pig, Foghorn Leghorn, Yosemite
Sam and Speedy Gonzalez. Mel Blanc also hosted an eponymous
"Mel Blanc Show". In this show, Mel speaks in his usual voice
(that of Sylvester The Cat) and plays the role of a fix-it shop
owner. Mel also voices the role of his assistant Zookie (who
speaks like Porky Pig but with more stutter). Mel's
unsuccessful attempts to impress the rich father of his fiancée
Betty forms the crux of most storylines.
```

Here is an extract from my vintage radio article.

> Mel Blanc was the voice behind popular cartoon characters such as Daffy Duck, Bugs Bunny, Porky Pig, Foghorn Leghorn, Yosemite Sam and Speedy Gonzalez. Mel Blanc also hosted an eponymous "Mel Blanc Show". In this show, Mel speaks in his usual voice (that of Sylvester The Cat) and plays the role of a fix-it shop owner. Mel also voices the role of his assistant Zookie (who speaks like Porky Pig but with more stutter). Mel's unsuccessful attempts to impress the rich father of his fiancée Betty forms the crux of most storylines.

# Two adjacent quoted lines - still one paragraph

A blockquote using multiple adjacent lines is only a reading and writing convenience. In the output, they appear as one paragraph.

```
>Mel Blanc was the voice behind popular cartoon characters such
as Daffy Duck, Bugs Bunny, Porky Pig, Foghorn Leghorn, Yosemite
Sam and Speedy Gonzalez. Mel Blanc also hosted an eponymous
"Mel Blanc Show".
>In this show, Mel speaks in his usual voice (that of Sylvester
The Cat) and plays the role of a fix-it shop owner. Mel also
voices the role of his assistant Zookie (who speaks like Porky
Pig but with more stutter). Mel's unsuccessful attempts to
impress the rich father of his fiancée Betty forms the crux of
most storylines.
```

> Mel Blanc was the voice behind popular cartoon characters such as Daffy Duck, Bugs Bunny, Porky Pig, Foghorn Leghorn, Yosemite Sam and Speedy Gonzalez. Mel Blanc also hosted an eponymous "Mel Blanc Show". In this show, Mel speaks in his usual voice (that of Sylvester The Cat) and plays the role of a fix-it shop owner. Mel also voices the role of his assistant Zookie (who speaks like Porky Pig but with more stutter). Mel's unsuccessful attempts to impress the rich father of his fiancée Betty forms the crux of most storylines.

# Two adjacent quoted lines with an empty line in between - two blockquotes

```
>Mel Blanc was the voice behind popular cartoon characters such
as Daffy Duck, Bugs Bunny, Porky Pig, Foghorn Leghorn, Yosemite
Sam and Speedy Gonzalez. Mel Blanc also hosted an eponymous
"Mel Blanc Show".

>In this show, Mel speaks in his usual voice (that of Sylvester
The Cat) and plays the role of a fix-it shop owner. Mel also
voices the role of his assistant Zookie (who speaks like Porky
Pig but with more stutter). Mel's unsuccessful attempts to
impress the rich father of his fiancée Betty forms the crux of
most storylines.
```

> Mel Blanc was the voice behind popular cartoon characters such as Daffy Duck, Bugs Bunny, Porky Pig, Foghorn Leghorn, Yosemite Sam and Speedy Gonzalez. Mel Blanc also hosted an

> eponymous "Mel Blanc Show".
>
> In this show, Mel speaks in his usual voice (that of Sylvester The Cat) and plays the role of a fix-it shop owner. Mel also voices the role of his assistant Zookie (who speaks like Porky Pig but with more stutter). Mel's unsuccessful attempts to impress the rich father of his fiancée Betty forms the crux of most storylines.

# Adjacent lines with quoted empty line in the middle - two paragraphs in one blockquote

```
>Mel Blanc was the voice behind popular cartoon characters such
as Daffy Duck, Bugs Bunny, Porky Pig, Foghorn Leghorn, Yosemite
Sam and Speedy Gonzalez. Mel Blanc also hosted an eponymous
"Mel Blanc Show".
>
>In this show, Mel speaks in his usual voice (that of Sylvester
The Cat) and plays the role of a fix-it shop owner. Mel also
voices the role of his assistant Zookie (who speaks like Porky
Pig but with more stutter). Mel's unsuccessful attempts to
impress the rich father of his fiancée Betty forms the crux of
most storylines.
```

> Mel Blanc was the voice behind popular cartoon characters such as Daffy Duck, Bugs Bunny, Porky Pig, Foghorn Leghorn, Yosemite Sam and Speedy Gonzalez. Mel Blanc also hosted an eponymous "Mel Blanc Show".
>
> In this show, Mel speaks in his usual voice (that of Sylvester The Cat) and plays the role of a fix-it shop owner. Mel also voices the role of his assistant Zookie (who speaks like Porky Pig but with more stutter). Mel's unsuccessful attempts to impress the rich father of his fiancée Betty forms the crux of most storylines.

# Blockquotes with more than just paragraphs

MarkDown can fail miserably with nested blockquotes and lists. CommonMark really shines here.

```
>[![www.vsubhash.com](http://www.vsubhash.in/sss-img/banner-
vsubhash-dotcom220.png)](http://www.vsubhash.com "Home Page")
>
```

```
>[V. Subhash.com](http://www.vsubhash.com)
>================
>
>Welcome to my ...
>
>Articles
>--------
>
> * CommonMark Quick Reference
> * 'FFMPEG Quick Hacks' book
> * '2020 Fresh Clean Jokes For Everyone' book
> * ...
>
>...
```

# V. Subhash.com

Welcome to my ...

## Articles

- CommonMark Quick Reference
- 'FFMPEG Quick Hacks' book
- '2020 Fresh Clean Jokes For Everyone' book
- ...

...

# Nested blockquotes

```
The first radio broadcast was made by a Canadian named Reginald
Fessenden on Christmas Eve in 1906. He was also the first one
to transmit human voice over radio in 1900. Until then radio
transmissions were Morse code messages. His wife Helen wrote:

>On Christmas Eve and New Year's Eve of 1906 the first
Broadcasting occurred. Three days in advance Reg had his
operators notify the ships of the U.S. Navy and of the United
Fruit Co. that were equipped with the Fessenden apparatus that
it was the intention of the Brant Rock Station to broadcast
speech, music and singing on those two evenings.
>
```

```
>Describing this, Fessenden wrote:
>>The program on Christmas Eve was as follows: first a short
speech by me saying what we were going to do, then some
phonograph music. The music on the phonograph being Handel's
'Largo'. Then came a violin solo by me, being a composition of
Gounod called 'O, Holy Night', and ending up with the words
'Adore and be still' of which I sang one verse, in addition to
playing on the violin, though the singing of course was not
very good. Then came the Bible text, 'Glory to God in the
highest and on earth peace to men of good will', and finally we
wound up by wishing them a Merry Christmas and then saying that
we proposed to broadcast again New Year's Eve.
```

The first radio broadcast was made by a Canadian named Reginald Fessenden on Christmas Eve in 1906. He was also the first one to transmit human voice over radio in 1900. Until then radio transmissions were Morse code messages. His wife Helen wrote:

> On Christmas Eve and New Year's Eve of 1906 the first Broadcasting occurred. Three days in advance Reg had his operators notify the ships of the U.S. Navy and of the United Fruit Co. that were equipped with the Fessenden apparatus that it was the intention of the Brant Rock Station to broadcast speech, music and singing on those two evenings.

Describing this, Fessenden wrote:

>> The program on Christmas Eve was as follows: first a short speech by me saying what we were going to do, then some phonograph music. The music on the phonograph being Handel's 'Largo'. Then came a violin solo by me, being a composition of Gounod called 'O, Holy Night', and ending up with the words 'Adore and be still' of which I sang one verse, in addition to playing on the violin, though the singing of course was not very good. Then came the Bible text, 'Glory to God in the highest and on earth peace to men of good will', and finally we wound up by wishing them a Merry Christmas and then saying that we proposed to broadcast again New Year's Eve.

# Lists

Lists are of two types:

1. ordered (numbered) lists and
2. unordered (unnumbered) lists.

## Ordered lists

Ordered list items should begin with a number, a full stop [ . ] or the closing curved bracket [ ) ] and a space.

```
1) Hydrogen
2) Helium
3) Lithium
4) Beryllium
```

1. Hydrogen
2. Helium
3. Lithium
4. Beryllium

## Unordered lists

Asterisks, hyphens and pluses can be be used to create unordered lists. Sub-list items must be preceded by two spaces.

```
* One two
  * Buckle my shoe
  * Three four
     - Open the door
     * Five six
  * Picking up sticks
    * Seven eight
    - Lay them straight
    - Nine ten
+ A big fat hen
```

- One two
  - Buckle my shoe
  - Three four
    - Open the door
    - Five six
  - Picking up sticks
    - Seven eight
    - Lay them straight
    - Nine ten
- A big fat hen

# Breaks inside list items

A list item can have multiple sub-list items. If two text lines in one list item are separated by an empty line, a new paragraph will be created for the second one. To have some text in the same paragraph but in the next line, end the first line with a backslash [ \ ] or two spaces.

```
* Noble gases
  * Helium\
    What did hydrogen say? "__He__ sounds funny."
  * Argon\
    This inert gas is used in fluorescent lighting.
  * Xenon\
    This element is used in powerful lamps and lasers.
* Halogens
  * Chlorine

    This element is used as a disinfectant.
  * Iodine

    This element is essential for the functioning of the
thyroid gland.
```

- Noble gases
  - Helium
    What did hydrogen say? "**He** sounds funny."
  - Argon
    This inert gas is used in fluorescent lighting.
  - Xenon
    This element is used in powerful lamps and lasers.
- Halogens
  - Chlorine

    This element is used as a disinfectant.

  - Iodine

    This element is essential for the functioning of the thyroid gland.

The content inside a list item are bound by the latter's boundaries and follow the same markdown rules as other content.

# HTML blocks

You can use HTML markup in your markdown. HTML markup that begins on a newline will be sent to the output document without being processed until a new empty new line is found.

## Unprocessed HTML

These HTML blocks begin on a new line. Placing markdown inside them is useless.

```
<p>One small step for<del> **a** </del> man; one giant leap for
mankind.</p>

<table>
  <tr><td>**First Name**</td><td>**Last Name**</td></tr>
  <tr><td>John</td><td>Doe</td></tr>
  <tr><td>Jane</td><td>Doe</td></tr>
</table>
```

One small step for ~~**a**~~ man; one giant leap for mankind.

**First Name** **Last Name**

| John | Doe |
| Jane | Doe |

## Processed HTML

Markdown content placed a new line from the HTML block will be processed as markdown.

```
One small step for<del> **a** </del> man; one giant leap for
mankind.

<table>
  <tr><td>

  **First Name**

  </td><td>

  **Last Name**

  </td></tr>
  <tr><td>John</td><td>Doe</td></tr>
  <tr><td>Jane</td><td>Doe</td></tr>
</table>
```

One small step for ~~a~~ man; one giant leap for mankind.

| **First Name** | **Last Name** |

| John | Doe |
| Jane | Doe |

As you can see, the cell contents in the first row have been converted to paragraphs. This has affected their formatting.

While you can use HTML within markdown, the reverse is not so seamless. Because of the restrictions and problems, it is not recommended.

# Exporting to other document formats

When you convert CommonMark to HTML using the CommonMark executable, the output HTML is generated on a strictly as-needed basis. This output does not constitute a 'valid' HTML document. A *valid* HTML document is necessary for converting CommonMark to other document formats.

## Exporting CommonMark as a valid HTML document

To illustrate this requirement, the following CommonMark text was used to generate the beginning of one of the annexure chapters.

```
Excerpts from
*2020 Fresh Clean Jokes For Kids*
---------------------------------

* **Can you say 100 words in one minute? None of the words
should have the letters A, B, C or D.**
  Zero, one, two, three, four... ninety-nine.

* **Phantom Hand Challenge**

  ![ESP](./images/esp.png#right)

  This is a prank you can play on others. Ask one of them to
hold out their arm as   shown in the picture. Place your
index and middle finger on the person's wrist and slowly walk
them towards the elbow pit. After you start, tell the person to
close his/her eyes and open it only when your fingers reach the
elbow pit. The person's brain will always be tricked into
thinking it has happened prematurely.

* **What is a politically incorrect name for a kid who tries to
explain his poor report card?**
  Activist.

* **What is a politically incorrect name for a parent who hides
the tin with sweets on the top shelf?**
  Elitist.

* **What is a politically incorrect name for a kid who eats the
sweets in the top shelf and then gets caught?**
  Pacifist.

...
```

The CommonMark executable generates the following HTML for the previous text.

```
<h2>Excerpts from<br />
```

```
<em>2020 Fresh Clean Jokes For Kids</em></h2>
<ul>
<li>
<p><strong>Can you say 100 words in one minute? None of the
words should have the letters A, B, C or D.</strong><br />
Zero, one, two, three, four... ninety-nine.</p>
</li>
<li>
<p><strong>Phantom Hand Challenge</strong></p>
<p><img src="./images/esp.png#right" alt="ESP" /></p>
<p>This is a prank you can play on others. Ask one of them to
hold out their arm as   shown in the picture. Place your index
and middle finger on the person's wrist and slowly walk them
towards the elbow pit. After you start, tell the person to
close his/her eyes and open it only when your fingers reach the
elbow pit. The person's brain will always be tricked into
thinking it has happened prematurely.</p>
</li>
<li>
<p><strong>What is a politically incorrect name for a kid who
tries to explain his poor report card?</strong><br />
Activist.</p>
</li>
<li>
<p><strong>What is a politically incorrect name for a parent
who hides the tin with sweets on the top shelf?</strong><br />
Elitist.</p>
</li>
<li>
<p><strong>What is a politically incorrect name for a kid who
eats the sweets in the top shelf and then gets caught?</strong>
<br />
Pacifist.</p>
</li>
...
```

As you can see, the output HTML does not form a valid HTML document. It is up to you to create it when needed.

For generating my books, I place the HTML generated by CommonMark between the BODY tags of a HTML document template.

```
<!doctype html>
<html>
  <head>
    <meta http-equiv="Content-Type" content="text/html;
charset=UTF-8" />
    <title>CommonMark Ready Reference</title>
    <style>
      h2 { font-family: 'Enterprise';   }
      p { font-family: 'Lato'; }
    </style>
  </head>
  <body>

  <!-- Drop HTML generated by CommonMark below -->


  <!-- Drop HTML generated by CommonMark above -->
```

```
    </body>
</html>
```

I have written a script (program) that combines the template with the output of the CommonMark executable. You can do the same manually using a text editor. The combined HTML will be a valid HTML document.

```
<!doctype html>
<html>
   <head>
      <meta http-equiv="Content-Type" content="text/html;
charset=UTF-8" />
      <title>CommonMark Ready Reference</title>
      <style>
        h2 { font-family: 'Enterprise';  }
        p { font-family: 'Lato'; }
      </style>
   </head>
   <body>

      <!-- Drop HTML generated by CommonMark below -->

      <h2>Excerpts from<br />
      <em>2020 Fresh Clean Jokes For Kids</em></h2>
      <ul>
      <li>
      <p><strong>Can you say 100 words in one minute? None of the
words should have the letters A, B, C or D.</strong><br />
      Zero, one, two, three, four... ninety-nine.</p>
      </li>
      <li>
      <p><strong>Phantom Hand Challenge</strong></p>
      <p><img src="./images/esp.png#right" alt="ESP" /></p>
      <p>This is a prank you can play on others. Ask one of them
to hold out their arm as   shown in the picture. Place your
index and middle finger on the person's wrist and slowly walk
them towards the elbow pit. After you start, tell the person to
close his/her eyes and open it only when your fingers reach the
elbow pit. The person's brain will always be tricked into
thinking it has happened prematurely.</p>
      </li>
      <li>
      <p><strong>What is a politically incorrect name for a kid
who tries to explain his poor report card?</strong><br />
      Activist.</p>
      </li>
      <li>
      <p><strong>What is a politically incorrect name for a
parent who hides the tin with sweets on the top shelf?</strong>
<br />
      Elitist.</p>
      </li>
      <li>
      <p><strong>What is a politically incorrect name for a kid
who eats the sweets in the top shelf and then gets caught?
</strong><br />
      Pacifist.</p>
      </li>
      <li>…</li>
      </ul>
```

```
    <!-- Drop HTML generated by CommonMark above -->

    </body>
</html>
```

A valid HTML document has a DOCTYPE declaration followed by a HTML tag. The HTML tag contains a HEAD tag and a BODY tag. The HEAD tag contain more tags that specify title, metadata, style (CSS), and interactive logic (JavaScript).

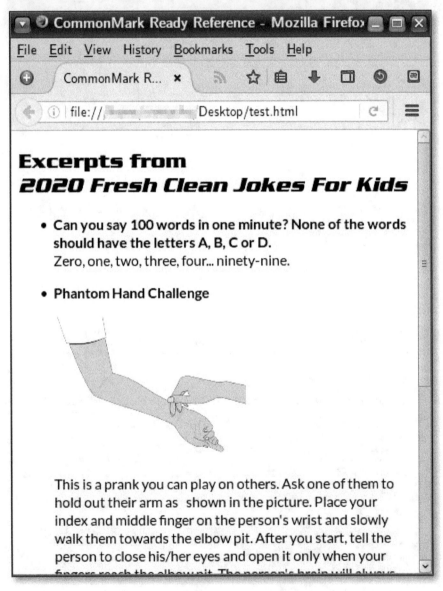

For the heck of it, go ahead and open the HTML document in

LibreOffice/OpenOffice/Word and save it in ODF (Open Document Format) or Word Doc format. *No problemente!*

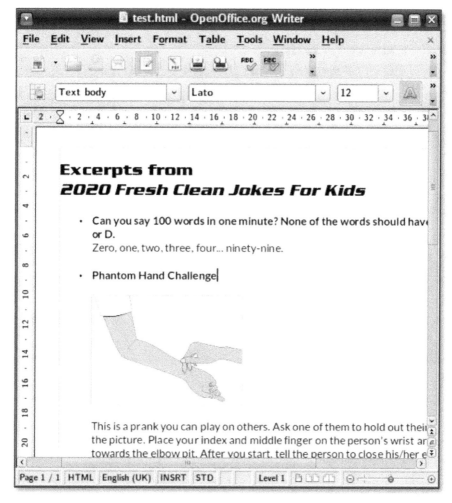

Although these editors export to PDF, you can open the HTML document in a browser and print to a PDF file. Printing to PDF with a browser requires a lot of custom printing setup changes but it can be done.

I generate a PDF version of my books using a software called KHTMLToPDF that mimics the Mozilla Firefox browser. It needs some programming and web-designing skills but offers more control. I use my stylized HTML document source in another software called Calibre to create ebooks in the EPUB format. This book and the more than two dozen books that I had published were all created using CommonMark.

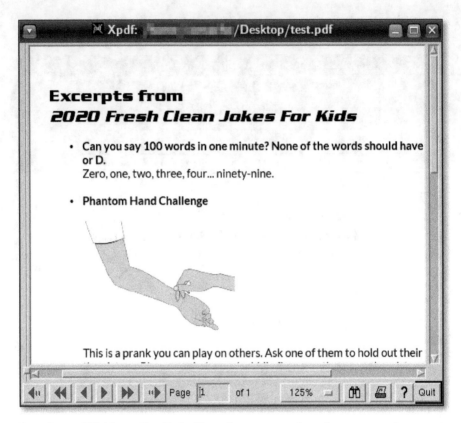

If you know CSS (Cascading Style Sheets), you can style or format your document very precisely. If you know Javascript, you can go even further. Javascript can be used to process content in a way that cannot be done through CommonMark. For example, in my 2020 jokebook, I used a JavaScript script to count the jokes. (Manually counting over 3000 jokes was not going to be easy.)

```
<!doctype html>
<html>
  <head>
    <meta http-equiv="Content-Type" content="text/html;
charset=UTF-8" />
    <title>2020 Fresh Clean Jokes For Everyone</title>
    <link rel="stylesheet" href="style.css" />
    <script>

      document.addEventListener("DOMContentLoaded",
loadHandler, false);

      function loadHandler() {
       try {
         countJokes();
       } catch (err) {
        console.error("Jokes2020: " + err);
       }
      }
```

```
      function countJokes() {
         // Logic to count jokes
      }
   </script>
</head>
<body>
...
```

For most people, Javascript is overkill. However, if you or someone else can do the CSS in the HTML, then that is the best. CSS-formatted HTML documents have numerous advantages over ODF or Word documents.

- All your output documents look the same.
- No need to worry about pagination and positioning.
- No errors introduced by the text editor (such the notorious Microsoft Word) as it tries to change 'simple quotations marks' to 'inverted quotation marks'.
- As a browser opens a HTML document in read-only mode, documents with lots of images are easier to scroll. The afore-mentioned Word program would become sluggish as it endlessly re-formats your document and also introduce unnecessary blank pages and section changes.

# Exporting to ODT, DOCX and PDF

LibreOffice has a command-line version. It can convert HTML files to its native format ODT, Microsoft Word DOCX and Adobe Acrobat PDF. If the HTML uses images, the ODT and DOCX files will only link to the images. To make the files truly portable, you need to first encode the images into the HTML. LibreOffice has an option for that.

```
cmark --unsafe --validate-utf8 \
      my-pages.md.txt > \
      my-pages.html

cat my-template.html my-pages.html > my-document.html
echo "</body></html>" >> my-document.html

libreoffice --convert-to "odt" "html:HTML:EmbedImages" \
            --outdir /tmp \
            my-document.html
libreoffice --convert-to "odt"  /tmp/my-document.html
libreoffice --convert-to "docx" my-document.odt
libreoffice --convert-to "pdf" my-document.odt
```

This kind of conversion takes only a few seconds or minutes. There is a caveat though. LibreOffice will remove CSS styling that it does not understand or feels is not necessary. Even then, it is great for automated document creation.

---

Well, you have finished the book. If you give it a good rating ( ☆ ☆ ☆ ☆ ☆ ) or review online, it would be much appreciated. If you have any corrections or suggestions, write to me at **Info@VSubhash.Com**.

Some of my titles are available for FREE on several ebook stores and library apps. Give them a try. I have written more than two dozen non-fiction books on a wide range of subjects. I have also written ONE fiction title(s)! Check the backlist for more details or visit: **www.VSubhash.IN/books.html**

# Puzzles from my book
# *World Of Word Ladders*

There are two books in this series for children, each with 100 word ladder puzzles. You need to change one letter in each rung and transform the first word into the last word. Conditions are that none of the words be a proper name, foreign (non-English) word or abbreviation.

## THREE-LETTER WORD LADDERS

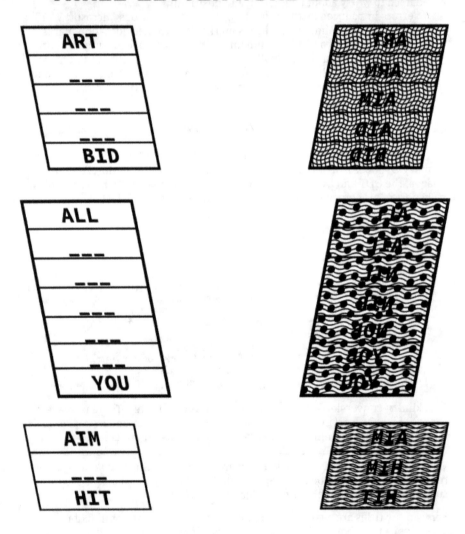

# FOUR-LETTER WORD LADDERS

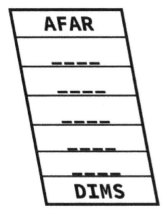

AFAR
____
____
____
____
____
DIMS

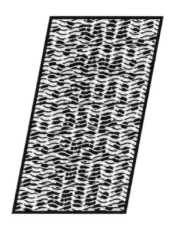

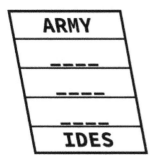

ARMY
____
____
____
IDES

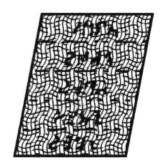

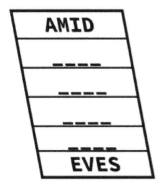

AMID
____
____
____
____
EVES

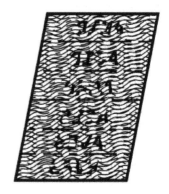

# Excerpts from 2020 Fresh Clean Jokes For Kids

- Can you say 100 words in one minute? None of the words should have the letters A, B, C or D.
  Zero, one, two, three, four... ninety-nine.

- **Phantom Hand Challenge**

  This is a prank you can play on others. Ask one of them to hold out their arm as   shown in the picture. Place your index and middle finger on the person's wrist and slowly walk them towards the elbow pit. After you start, tell the person to close his/her eyes and open it only when your fingers reach the elbow pit. The person's brain will always be tricked into thinking it has happened prematurely.

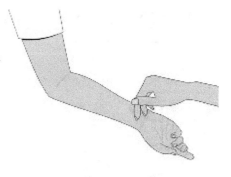

- **What is a politically incorrect name for a kid who tries to explain his poor report card?**
  Activist.

- **What is a politically incorrect name for a parent who hides the tin with sweets on the top shelf?**
  Elitist.

- What is a politically incorrect name for a kid who eats the sweets in the top shelf and then gets caught?
  Pacifist.

- What is a politically incorrect name for a sibling who finds the sweets in the top shelf before you can?
  Thought criminal.

- What is a politically incorrect name for a sibling who can reach the sweets in the top shelf?
  Height criminal.

- What is a politically incorrect name for an older sibling who prevents you from reaching the sweets in the top shelf?
  Obstructionist.

- What is a politically incorrect name that a parent calls you when you get caught and your story changes each time you tell it?
  Revisionist.

- What is a politically incorrect name for a sibling who is too chicken to get into trouble or does not get caught often enough?
  Conformist.

- What is a politically incorrect name for a sibling who always has a backup plan?
  Escapologist.

- What is a politically incorrect name for a sibling who does get caught but does not get punished as often as you do?
  Expert.

- What is a politically incorrect name for a sibling who manages eliminate his tracks before you bring it to your parents' attention?
  Survivalist.

- What is a politically incorrect name for a sibling whose problem-escaping skills have improved from pacifist to escapologist really quickly?
  Evolutionist.

- What is a politically incorrect name for an older sibling who steals stuff from you and gives them to his friends for free?
  Socialist.

- What is a politically incorrect name for an older sibling who always promises to return the stuff he has stolen from you but never does?
  Futurologist.

- What is a politically incorrect name for a sibling who is too chicken to get into trouble and when you get into trouble he is there to tell you 'I told you so'?
  Moralist.

- What is a politically incorrect name for a sibling who comes up with a plausible excuse for any situation?
  Innovator or child prodigy.

- **What is a politically incorrect name for a sibling who can get in and out of trouble without the slightest damage whatsoever?**
Constitutionalist.

- **What is a politically incorrect name for a sibling who backs up your version of the story?**
Loyalist.

- **What is a politically incorrect name for a sibling who rats on you?**
Populist.

- **What is a politically incorrect name for a sibling who rats on you and also correctly explains the motive?**
Conspiracy theorist.

- **What is a politically incorrect name for a sibling who rats on you, explains the motive and backs it up with proof?**
Crazy conspiracy theorist.

- **What is a politically incorrect name for a sibling who rats on you with extreme attention to detail?**
Archeologist.

- **What is a politically incorrect name for a sibling who tells your parent the exact differences between what you promised and what you actually did?**
Perfectionist.

- **What is a politically incorrect name for a sibling who rats on you with exaggerated detail?**
Inflationist.

- **What is a politically incorrect name for a sibling who pokes holes in your 'cover' story?**
Acupuncturist.

- **What is a politically incorrect name for a sibling who ratted on you and failed but made your parents not trust you anymore?**
Controversialist.

- **What is a politically incorrect name for a sibling who threatens to rat on you but is ready to offer you a deal?**
Mercantilist.

- **What is a politically incorrect name for a sibling who offered you a deal and then ratted on you?**
Dichotomist.

- **What is a politically incorrect name for a sibling who does not believe in the statute of limitations and continues to extort stuff citing crimes committed long ago?**
Imperialist.

- **What is a politically incorrect name for a sibling who threatens to rat on you and refuses to cut a deal?**
Antimaterialist.

- **What is a politically incorrect name for a sibling who does not just rat on**

you but also tells about your threats to use force?
Antimilitarist.

- What is a politically incorrect name for a sibling who does not just rat on you but also tells about your use of force?
  Victimologist.

- What is a politically incorrect name for a sibling who whittles down the crime despite your best efforts to exaggerate it?
  Abstractionist.

- What is a politically incorrect name for an older sibling who forces you into his crime when you threaten to rat on him?
  Neocolonialist.

- What is a politically incorrect name for a sibling who rats on your attempts to subjugate him?
  Abolitionist.

- What is a politically incorrect name for a sibling who threatens to rat on another sibling who threatened to rat on you?
  Salvationist.

- What is a politically incorrect name for a parent who refuses to believe your spin of the story?
  Subjectivist.

- What is a politically incorrect name for a parent who does not want to hear your legitimate excuses?
  Russophobe.

# Books By V. Subhash

I invite you to visit my site **WWW.VSUBHASH.IN**, and check out my other books, special discounts, sample PDFs and full ebooks. In 2020, I started publishing books. For two decades before that, I have been publishing feature articles, free ebooks (old editions still available), software (server/desktop/mobile), reviews (books, films, music and travel), funny memes and cartoons. You can follow these adventures on my blog: **http://www.vsubhash.in/blogs/blog/index.html**

My books for children are under the pseudonym **Ólafía L. Óla** (because it has laugh and LOL).

## 2020 Fresh Clean Jokes For Everyone

This is one of the biggest jokebooks ever written - over 3200 jokes spread over:

- *Part 1 — For Learning* (computer jokes, programming jokes, physics jokes, chemistry jokes, biology jokes, medical jokes, financial jokes, geography jokes, pun jokes and THREE CHAPTERS DEVOTED TO FOREIGN LANGUAGES)
- *Part 2 — For Fun* (bar jokes, blonde jokes, cross-the-road jokes, knock-knock jokes, lightbulb jokes, knock-knock jokes, romantic (breakup) jokes)
- *Part 3 — Only For Intellectuals* (jokes about philosophy, advertising, news and politics)

It has lots of jokes purely for the hedonist consumption of humour, content to improve vocabulary and general knowledge, thought-provoking poems (mostly as financial/political limericks set to the tune of popular nursery rhymes) AND some of the best one-liners EVER written in English. Absolutely no ( ˣ ) humour.

• Pages: 292    • Paperback: $10    • Ebook: An older subset with 420 jokes is available FOR FREE

## 2020 Fresh Clean Jokes For Kids

This 'for kids' subset of the 2020 jokebook has over 2200 jokes. It has all of *Part 1 (For Learning)* and some non-political jokes from *Part 2 (For Fun)* & *Part 3 (Only For Intellectuals)*. Joke types include computer jokes, programming jokes, cross-the-road jokes, physics jokes, chemistry jokes, biology jokes, medical jokes, financial jokes, geography jokes, knock-knock jokes, breakup jokes...). Special chapters include *Elephant & Ant Jokes* , *Off-The-Wall Philosophers*, *Useful French Phrases* , *Useful Latin Phrases* , *Other Useful Foreign Phrases* , *Jokes You Love To Hate* , *Jokes In Advertising* , and *Fancy Creature Jokes* . No political or controversial jokes. Absolutely no ( ˣ ) humour.

• Pages: 166    • Paperback: ₹550 or $7.70    • Ebook: Will never be published

## Ólafía L. Óla's Favourite Traditional Nursery Rhymes (Illustrated)

The political correctness pandemic has caused many nursery rhymes to be rewritten or eliminated altogether. This illustrated children's book has **50 popular English nursery rhymes in their traditional form**. The selected rhymes have stood the test of time and this **large-print paperback with edge-to-edge colour** makes it easy for kids to read them.

• Pages: 44 (39 with real content)    • Colour Paperback: $9

## Animalia Humorosum

This is an illustrated children's storybook based on Aesop's Fables. The stories have been made more believable by changing the ending with a humorous twist. **The book is a large-print paperback with edge-to-edge colour**.

• Pages: 30 (26 with real content)  • Colour Paperback: $9  • Ebook (for parental review): ₹70 or FREE

## World of Word Ladders

A word ladder has a diagram of a ladder with a word on both the first and last rungs. You need to change only one letter in the blank middle rungs so that the first word is transformed into the last word. Your words CANNOT be proper nouns, abbreviations, or loan or slang words.

Word ladders are a wonderful pastime. These puzzles are neither tough nor easy. They have the right balance between exercising the brain and having fun.

• Puzzles: 100 • Paperback: $6 (per volume)

## Vastu Shastra Explained

Vastu Shastra Explained is a plain-English Vástu Śastra building-architecture guide for those who wish to draw their own Vastu-compliant house plans. The book does not upsell Vaastu as a panacea for all ills nor does it portray Vastu as the Indian Feng Shui. Instead, it presents Vastu as a collection of time-tested best-practices in Indian building architecture.

• Pages: 40 (30 with real content)  • Colour Paperback: $7.77  • Ebook: ₹100

## Learn To Ride A Motorcycle In Five Minutes

Yes, you can! For most of my life, I did not know how to ride a motorbike. But, when I had to do, it took me only five minutes. On my first ride on my first bike, I travelled nearly 100 kilometres, across two cities and one national highway. Acquiring the skill takes less than five minutes and honing it will require a few weeks.

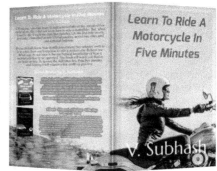

• Pages: 40 (30 with real content)
• Paperback: $7.70  • Ebook: ₹100

## How To Invest In Stocks, 2nd Edition

The first edition book was written in 2003 for the Indian stockmarket. It was popular around the world because it was a plain-English guide to investing in the stockmarket. The 2020 completely revised second edition maintains the original premise but has a global focus, updated information and new chapters. **It has some useful 'extra' information that you will not find in any investment book and no business school will teach you.** Mere book knowledge about stockmarkets will not help you understand the markets. Markets are influenced by news and information (there is a difference).

• Pages: 94  • Paperback: $9.90  • Ebook: ₹100 or FREE

## Email Newsletter Strategies For Profit

An organically grown mailing list is an invaluable resource for your business. It is your own social network. You need to nurture it like a baby. This book not only explains how to create user-friendly email newsletters but also helps you improve email deliverability, organically grow your mailing list, implement industry-standard best-practices and apply practical troubleshooting tips and tricks.

• Pages: 40 (33 with real content)  • Paperback: $7.70  • Ebook: ₹100

## How To Cure Common Cold

Non-allergic rhinitis or common cold is an ailment that usually resolves on its own. It can be very disruptive and make you feel miserable. *How To Cure Common Cold* **describes several palliative measures** (not curative options) that can be used to treat the symptoms while the body fights off the infection. Because this is a thin topic, **bonus content** on natural weight-loss techniques, an easy-to-cook vegetarian food recipe, dental care tips, skincare tips, and some family-planning advice are included in this book. **DISCLAIMER**: The author is not a medical professional. Despite seeking medical treatment for common cold, his deviated nasal septum made the episodes very difficult to go through. Over several years, he tried and tested several palliative measures to treat the symptoms. In this book, he describes what measures might work for young healthy individuals like him. These recommendations are not intended for kids, adolescents, convalescents, seniors or in people where the cold symptoms are part of a larger ailment. **This book is not sponsored by any drug firm or commercial entity.**

• Pages: 31 (8 with real content)  • Paperback: $4.99  • Ebook: ₹99 or FREE

## The Devil's Dictionary

*The Devil's Dictionary* by Ambrose Bierce from 1911 is a great repository of brutally frank and unusually cynical descriptions for popular words and phrases in English. In my 2020 remake, the original text has been illustrated with contemporary caricatures (of Alexandria Ocasio Cortez, Bill Gates, Don Lemon, Elon Musk, Joe Biden...). It has the **neat easy-on-the-eye look of any new dictionary (modern fonts, two-column pages, starting/ending words on every page)**. If you consider yourself as a woke, liberal, Leftie, Progressive, Socialist, Communist, Feminist... then this book is not for you. This book by Bierce is a product of its time and may not match your unrealistic expectations. Maybe, you could gift it to your (fr)enemies. They might like it.

• Pages: 160  • Paperback: $9  • Ebook: ₹100

## Quick Start Guide to FFmpeg

**FFmpeg** is THE BEST software to easily create, edit, enhance and convert audio and video files. It is a FREE and open-source command-utility available **for Linux, Mac and Windows**. And, *Quick Start Guide to FFmpeg* is THE BEST book for an extensive FFmpeg tutorial, hack collection and quick reference. It is richly illustrated with color screenshots, code examples and tables to help you work with audio, video, images, animations, fonts, subtitles and metadata like a PRO. NOTE: In 2023, the old self-published book *FFmpeg Quick Hacks* was withdrawn.

• Pages: 280   • Colour Paperback: $44.99   • PDF Ebook: $29.99 (from Apress/SpringerNature)

## CommonMark Ready Reference

MarkDown is an easy human-readable text format that can serve as the common base for exporting to multiple document formats such as HTML, ODF, DOC/DOCX, PDF and ebook (EPUB, MOBI…). It is a great tool for authors, technical writers and content developers to create books, manuals, web pages and other rich-text content. CommonMark is a new well-formed standard for the old MarkDown spec. **CommonMark was one of the reasons I was able to write and design 21 books in one year.** Incidentally, this is the first-ever book on CommonMark. You will be buying a piece of history! The paperback's covers are designed like a quick reference card.

• Pages: 56 (39 with real content, 6 with bonus content)   • Paperback: $6   • Ebook: ₹100 or FREE

## Linux Command-Line Tips & Tricks

This is a tips-and-tricks collection for Linux command-line warriors. It is also at an advanced level. It assumes that you already know how to use the terminal and are adept at shell programming. It does not teach you the basics or try to be a comprehensive reference. It trusts your intuition and focuses on things you are most likely to forget. Because of its ancient history, BASH scripting has some odd programming constructs that are difficult to memorize. This book tries to provide a ready-reference for such archaic but crucial details. It pays special attention to coding mistakes or unusual circumstances in which your script or command will fail. The paperback has screenshots and syntax-highlighted code examples, all in full-colour.

• Pages: 100   • Colour Paperback: $9.99   • Ebook: ₹100 or FREE

## PC Hardware Explained

You can build a PC in 30 minutes with just a screwdriver. Knowing which computer components will work together is not so easy. This full-colour paperback will explain computer hardware using **simple terms, illustrations, photographs and tables**. Before **buying a new laptop from the store** or **assembling a new desktop from parts**, get this book. You will be able to read the technical specifications of a PC and understand what it can and cannot do. The mumbo-jumbo accompanying the sales pitch of a new computer will not be so alien.

• Pages: 30 (22 with real content)   • Colour paperback: $7   • Ebook: ₹100

## Cool Electronic Projects

If you are learning electronics or thinking of it as a future hobby, this FULL-COLOUR book has some fun projects to begin with. They will not waste your time or money, will be extremely useful (particularly in emergencies) and are quite easy to make. Just one of these projects uses AC (alternating current). The rest work on DC (direct current) and are safe for kids (if you think soldering is safe). These projects are good for the environment too, as they reuse electronic parts that would have been discarded. If you are a survivalist, then you will be happy that all the projects will run off-the-grid, as they can consume renewable energy. For the tinkerer, there are projects that add MORE POWER than what the manufacturer had provided. For the parent of lazy children, there are annoying alarms that can wake up the dead.

• Pages: 40 (33 with real content)   • Paperback: $9.90   • Ebook: ₹100

## How To Install Solar

This is a heavily illustrated guidebook for **INDIAN** solar power enthusiasts, DIY hacks, home-owners and electricians about solar panels, batteries, inverters, charge controllers, installation procedures and costs. It starts with a simple introduction to home electrical systems, proceeds on to describe various aspects of solar power and options available for home owners, and then provides step-by-step instructions for installing a low-cost DC-only solar charge controller system for ₹6000 and a solar inverter system providing AC power backup for ₹30,000. Also included is an extensive FAQs section based on questions and reviews published by solar power users online.

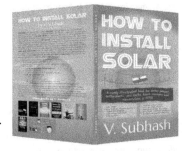

• Pages: 76   • Colour paperback: $7.70   • Ebook: ₹100

## Unlikely Stories

This is an anthology of horror and comedy stories **based on real incidents**. After writing so many non-fiction books, I was **forced by governments of several nations** to name this book as 'Unlikely Stories' and release it only as a fiction title (!) with this rather quaint description (verbatim copy):

> Boy meets girl. Both fall in love. Boy proposes marriage. Girl postpones decision for one month. Girl's gonna leave next day. Until then, boy tries to impress girl by telling stories — funny stories... scary stories... and all kinds in between. No worries. Everything ends well.
>
> The stories were tough to come by. Having given up on fiction years ago, the young man had to marshal some old personal anecdotes, wild tales told by strangers, and even some vividly detailed nightmares for his first novel. Like a male Scheherazade, he somehow wove those yarns together. They also just about helped him bag his babe.

As a result, the stories are mostly **supernatural/paranormal fantasies with ample doses of action, horror, humour and sci-fi**. The entire book is in first person and everything happens very fast. There is never a dull moment.

- **The trip**: The lead is invited by his friend to spend the weekend at a resort. There, he meets the first heroine **Vampira**. That is not her real name.
- **The swim**: The lead decides that *Vampira* is the soul mate he has been waiting for all his life. He tells several stories to entertain his friend's kids and also impress Vampira.
- **The exorcist**: The second lead is an Indian scamster who escapes to the US to start a new life. He attempts to go legit but finds competition from a professional medium operating under the trade name of **Mademoiselle Zuma**. (She is dangerous because she is secretly a mind-reader.) He is forced to try his hand at performing an exorcism that the Church has given up on.
- **Alien encounter**: After the successful exorcism, this lead is asked to help a teenager who has been repeatedly 'abducted' by an 'alien'. This story also includes a scientifically accurate discussion that convincingly proves the impossibility of alien presence on Earth and the 100% likelihood of all UFOs and alien abductions being staged by governments. Hopefully, this story will help victims of these frauds achieve some sort of explanation or closure to their harrowing experiences.
- **The lift**: A recently deceased security guard haunts a lift where he had died and seeks revenge.
- **Femme fatale**: The second lead has a showdown with a female animal spirit.
- **The seance**: A young woman in the city is troubled by nightmares involving a hooded skeleton. A newly married nurse in a rural area blanks out every night. She is also troubled by bizarre nightmares. Mademoiselle Zuma solves both cases.
- **The haunting**: An old mansion is haunted by a presence. Every new buyer and his family gets driven to such desperation that they eventually sell. The current owner wants the paranormal activities investigated. The second lead tries and almost gets killed.
- **Family planning**: The first lead and Vampira plan their life together. In the first ending, they get married. In the second ending (written by the lead after their first night), **Stone Age Man (SAM)** and **Stone Age Woman (SAW)** discover some truths about the mystery of life. (This is an over-the-top parody of the **controversy about** *MEN WRITING WOMEN* .) Other than these intimate events implied in comic fashion, there is no physical contact between the sexes in the entire book. Not even a kiss. It is clean throughout. (The attractive elf on the cover is on the lines of James Hadley Chase covers but nothing more. She does exist in one of the stories as a scary animal spirit.) No corny mushy dialogue. No degeneracy. No weirdness. Just no low-hanging fruit (that seems to be the staple fare today).

**WARNING**: The 1st edition has content toxic (… lots of unrestrained *mansplaining* that is very *triggering*) to woke individuals. If you are one, do not read it and be disappointed. Get the 2nd edition instead. It may be available in 2023. The woke-toxic content has been mostly removed to make room for new content. 'Mostly' because I do not care or believe in *THE CURRENT THING* .

Second-edition stories are mostly written from the perspective of Zuma.

- **Shadows in the night**: A young woman is troubled by a ghostly intruder at night.
- **Zuma vs. Cutie**: Zuma finds competition from an unlikely friend. She and her husband are asked to help rescue a kidnapped boy.
- **The evil twin**: A rich heiress is driven to desperation by a deceased twin who wants her to die too.
- **The alien invasion**: A huge bolide crashes down in the Atlantic. The site becomes an alien platform for launching attacks on USA, Canada, Australia and New Zealand. The aliens do not attack any other nation. The US government and military collapse after a few days. The strangest thing about the invasion is that the alien's primary objective is not humans but cows.

  While this story will describe the alien invasion in plain English, it will also provide a viable economic model for a successful alien invasion.

• 1st edition paperback (140 small grayscale pages): $9   • 2nd edition paperback (150 bigger colour pages): $20   • 1st edition ebook: ₹100   • 2nd edition ebook: Will not be published

# About the author

**V. Subhash** is an invisible Indian writer, programmer and cartoonist. In 2020, he published one of the biggest jokebooks of all time and then followed it up with a tech book on FFmpeg and a 400-page volume of 149 political cartoons. Although he had published a few ebooks as early as 2003, Subhash did not publish books in the traditional sense until 2020. For over two decades, Subhash had used his website **www.VSubhash.com** as the main outlet for his writing. During this time, he had accumulated a lot of published and unpublished material. This content and the automated book-production process that he had developed helped him publish 21 books in his first year. In February 2023, Apress (SpringerNature) published his rewritten and updated FFmpeg book as *QUICK START GUIDE TO FFMPEG*. Thus, by early 2023, Subhash had published 30 books! In 2022, Subhash ran out of non-fiction material and tried his hand at fiction. The result was *UNLIKELY STORIES*, a collection of horror and comedy short stories. After adding new stories to this fiction title (for its second edition), Subhash plans to pause his writing and move on to other things. Subhash pursues numerous hobbies and interests, several of which have become the subject of his books such as *COOL ELECTRONIC PROJECTS*, *HOW TO INSTALL SOLAR* and *HOW TO INVEST IN STOCKS*. He was inspired to write his gigantic jokebook after years of listening to vintage American radio shows such as *Fibber & Molly* and *Duffy's Tavern*.

# CommonMark/MarkDown Quick Reference
## from WWW.VSUBHASH.IN

### Text

**Bold** *Italic* ***Bold-Italic***

**Bold** *Italic* ***Bold-Italic***

```
<strong>Bold</strong> <em>Italic</em> <em>
<strong>Bold-Italic</strong></em>
```

### Line Break

```
One  Two
Buckle My  Shoe
```

One Two
Buckle My Shoe

```
<p>One Two<br />Buckle My Shoe</p>
```

### Horizontal Rule (Line)

```
Three underscores

___

is a line
```

Three underscores
___
is a line

```
<p>Three underscores</p><hr /><p>is a line</p>
```

### Code Block

````
```
int main() {
 printf("Hello, World!");
 return(0);
}
```
````

```
int main() {
 printf("Hello, World!");
 return(0);
}
```

```
<pre><code>int main() {
 printf("Hello, World!");
 return(0);
}
</code></pre>
```

### Code Span

Day: `20 February, 2020`

Day: 20 February, 2020

```
Day: <code>20 February, 2020</code>
```

### Image

```
![RT.com](http://www.rt.com/logo.gif)
```

**RT**

```
<img src="http://www.rt.com/logo.gif"
alt="RT.com" />
```

### Link

```
[www.rt.com](http://www.rt.com "RT.com")
```

www.rt.com

```
<a href="http://www.rt.com"
title="RT.com">www.rt.com</a>
```

### Headings

```
# Heading 1
## Heading 2
### Heading 3
#### Heading 4
##### Heading 5
###### Heading 6
```

# Heading 1
## Heading 2
### Heading 3
#### Heading 4
##### Heading 5
###### Heading 6

```
<h1>Heading 1</h1><h2>Heading 2</h2><h3>Heading 3</h3>
<h4>Heading 4</h4><h5>Heading 5</h5><h6>Heading 6</h6>
```

### Lists

```
1. One          * He
2. Two          * She
3. Three        * It
```

1. One
2. Two
3. Three

- He
- She
- It

```
<ol><li>One</li>        <ul><li>He</li>
<li>Two</li>            <li>She</li>
<li>Three</li></ol>     <li>It</li></ul>
```

## Books by V. Subhash

## Citations

By the [1920s][nbc], commercial radio networks run by the National Broadcasting Corporation (NBC) had become popular. Although the television was invented in the 1930s, it did not take off as factories and materials were diverted for war production. Thus, radio enjoyed two decades as the most popular medium for news and entertainment. These decades are known as the *[golden age of radio][golden_age]*. After World War II, TV displaced radio in popularity. Radio then served a niche - people on their commute. In the age of the Internet...


[nbc]: #nbc
[golden_age]: #golden_age

---

###### References

 * <span id="nbc"></span>
   National Broadcasting Company history files - <https://lccn.loc.gov/2002660093>
 * <span id="golden_age"></span>
   Golden Age of American radio -
   <http://www.britannica.com/topic/Golden-Age-of-American-radio>

---

By the 1920s, commercial radio networks run by the National Broadcasting Corporation (NBC) had become popular. Although the television was invented in the 1930s, it did not take off as factories and materials were diverted for war production. Thus, radio enjoyed two decades as the most popular medium for news and entertainment. These decades are known as the *golden age of radio*. After World War II, TV displaced radio in popularity. Radio then served a niche - people on their commute. In the age of the Internet...

### References

- National Broadcasting Company history files - https://lccn.loc.gov/2002660093
- Golden Age of American radio - http://www.britannica.com/topic/Golden-Age-of-American-radio

---

```html
<p>By the <a href="#nbc">1920s, commercial radio networks run by the National Broadcasting Corporation (NBC) had become popular. Although the television was invented in the 1930s, it did not take off as factories and materials were diverted for war production. Thus, radio enjoyed two decades as the most popular medium for news and entertainment. These decades are known as the <em><a href="#golden_age">golden age of radio</a></em>. After World War II, TV displaced radio in popularity. Radio then served a niche - people on their commute. In the age of the Internet...</p> <p>...</p> <hr /> <h6>References</h6> <ul> <li><span id="nbc"></span> National Broadcasting Company history files - <a href="https://lccn.loc.gov/2002660093">https://lccn.loc.gov/2002660093</a></li> <li><span id="golden_age"></span> Golden Age of American radio - <a href="http://www.britannica.com/topic/Golden-Age-of-American-radio">http://www.britannica.com/topic/Golden-Age-of-American-radio</a>
```

## Blockquote

```
To wit, he said:
>CommonMark hit the ground with a well-defined standard from Day 1 and is set to replace and
overtake MarkDown. StackOverFlow.com and other sites have already adopted it.

And, it is true too!
```

To wit, he said:

> CommonMark hit the ground with a well-defined standard from Day 1 and is set to replace and overtake MarkDown. StackOverFlow.com and other sites have already adopted it.

And, it is true too!

```html
<p>To wit, he said:</p> <blockquote> <p>CommonMark hit the ground with a well-defined standard from Day 1 and is set to replace and overtake MarkDown. StackOverFlow.com and other sites have already adopted it.</p> </blockquote> <p>And, it is true too!</p>
```

www.ingramcontent.com/pod-product-compliance
Lightning Source LLC
La Vergne TN
LVHW051750050326
832903LV00029B/2827